Our Wonderful World of... FOOD

By Rebecca Phillips-Bartlett

KidHaven
PUBLISHING

Published in 2024 by
KidHaven Publishing, an Imprint of Greenhaven Publishing, LLC
2544 Clinton St., Buffalo, NY 14224

© 2023 BookLife Publishing Ltd.

Written by: Rebecca Phillips-Bartlett
Edited by: Elise Carraway
Designed by: Amy Li

Photo Credits

Images are courtesy of Shutterstock.com—with thanks to Getty Images, Thinkstock Photo, and iStockphoto. Recurring images – Anne Punch, Olga1818. Cover – cosmaa, happy.designer, INSdesign, sonelle.vdm, richardwibi, Zhe Vasylieva, VectorPot, Tatahnka, unturtle, Bika Ambon, Serbinka, Colorcocktail, Globe Turner, charnsitr, T. Lesia, G7 Stock. 2–3 – fatih likoglu. 4–5 – noir_illustration, Djent. 6–7 – Oleh Svetiukha, Alexandr III, Kenishirotie, Sudowoodo, The Jon Fernandez, Vector Posters and Cards, WS-Studio. 8–9 – Chatham172, Marcos Castillo, MaryDesy. 10–11 – jrslompo, Paulrommer SL, rafastockbr, Studio Aline Fernandes, VectoRaith. 12–13 – bonchan, konggraphic, Nsit, Olga1818, V. Matthiesen. 14–15 – BBA Photography, LineTale, Paul_Brighton, Vector_Up. 16–17 – charnsitr, Halil ibrahim mescioglu, Nsit, Rachael Arnott, Timolina, Yoko Design. 18–19 – asmiphotoshop, Natthapol Siridech, ONYXprj, robuart, teleginatania. 20–21 – Dernkadel, Fernlee, mamaruru, YUCALORA. 22–23 – StellaArts.

Cataloging-in-Publication Data

Names: Phillips-Bartlett, Rebecca, 1999-.
Title: Food / Rebecca Phillips-Bartlett.
Description: Buffalo, New York: KidHaven Publishing, 2024. | Series: Our wonderful world of… | Includes glossary and index.
Identifiers: ISBN 9781534546202 (pbk.) | ISBN 9781534546219 (library bound) | ISBN 9781534546226 (ebook)
Subjects: LCSH: Food--Juvenile literature. | Nutrition--Juvenile literature.
Classification: LCC TX355.P487 2024 | DDC 641.3--dc23

All rights reserved.
No part of this book may be reproduced in any form without permission in writing from the publisher, except by a reviewer.

Manufactured in the United States of America

CPSIA compliance information: Batch #CW24KH: For further information contact Greenhaven Publishing LLC at 1-844-317-7404.

Please visit our website, www.greenhavenpublishing.com.
For a free color catalog of all our high-quality books, call toll free 1-844-317-7404 or fax 1-844-317-7405.

Find us on

CONTENTS

Page 4	Welcome to Our Wonderful World!
Page 6	The United States
Page 8	Mexico
Page 10	Brazil
Page 12	Italy
Page 14	South Africa
Page 16	Türkiye
Page 18	India
Page 20	Japan
Page 22	A World of Fantastic Food
Page 24	Glossary and Index

Words that look like this can be found in the glossary on page 24.

WELCOME TO OUR WONDERFUL WORLD!

All around the world, people eat lots of fantastic food. Different countries grow, make, and enjoy many different types of food.

We are going on a <u>tour</u> around the world. In each country, we will meet a guide. They will tell us about the foods that are eaten in their country.

DID YOU KNOW?

Rice is one of the most popular foods in the world.

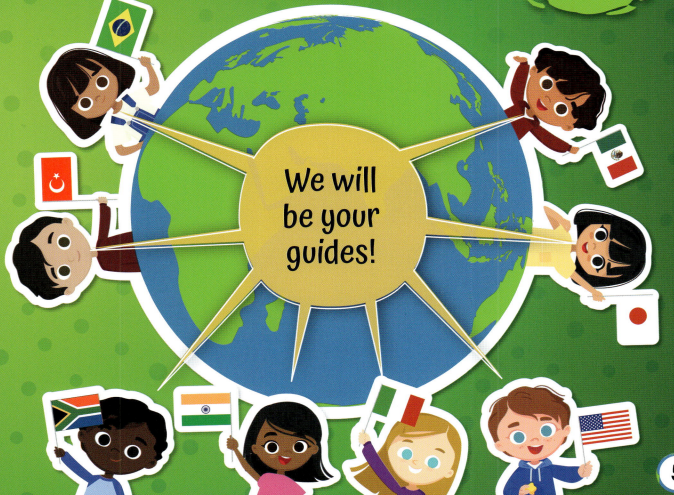

We will be your guides!

THE UNITED STATES

Key Lime Pie

Key lime pie is a sweet, creamy pie made with limes. This pie gets its name from a part of the U.S. state of Florida called the Florida Keys.

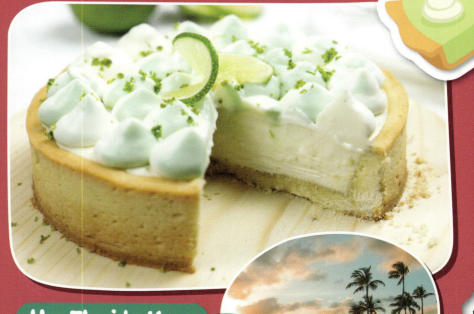

the Florida Keys

Hi, I am Rory. I live in the U.S.

Hot Dogs

A hot dog is a sausage most commonly served in a bun. Across the country, many places have added their own twist. Some places add different toppings, such as chili, mustard, or onions.

MEXICO

Hello! My name is Mateo. I live in Mexico.

Tacos

Tacos are a type of Mexican street food. Tacos are made with a flatbread called a tortilla. The tortilla is folded and filled with toppings such as meat, cheese, and vegetables.

Chiles en Nogada

Chiles en nogada are peppers that have been filled with meat, dried fruit, and spices. The peppers are covered with a white cream sauce. Chiles en Nogada are the same colors as the Mexican flag.

BRAZIL

Hi! I am Julianna. I live in Brazil.

Beijinhos

Beijinhos are a popular treat at birthday parties in Brazil. These bite-sized sweets are made of condensed milk, coconut, and butter. In English, "beijinho" means "little kiss."

Coxinhas

Coxinhas are small, crispy snacks. They are normally filled with shredded chicken. The filling is wrapped in <u>dough</u>. Then, the coxinhas are <u>fried</u>. They are crispy on the outside and soft on the inside.

ITALY

Arancini

Arancini are rice balls. They are filled with cheese and often meat or vegetables. Then, they are covered in breadcrumbs and fried. Once they are cooked, they look like oranges.

Hi, I am Sofia. I live in Italy.

DID YOU KNOW?

"Arancini" is the Sicilian word for "little oranges."

Margherita Pizza

Pizza is popular in many countries, but the first pizzas came from Italy. Italian pizza has a thin base with crispy edges. Margherita pizza is topped with tomato sauce, cheese, and basil leaves.

SOUTH AFRICA

Bobotie

Bobotie is made with minced meat and a creamy egg topping. It also has dried fruits and spices, so it tastes sweet and savory.

Hello! My name is Lethabo. I live in South Africa.

Bunny Chow

Bunny chow is an Indian curry served inside a loaf of bread. It is most popular in the city of Durban, where there are many examples of Indian culture.

Türkiye

Hi, I am Yusuf. I live in Türkiye.

Baklava

Baklava is a sweet, nutty dessert. It is made using very thin layers of yufka dough. Baklava is filled with nuts and soaked in syrup.

Kebabs

Kebabs are made of meat that is most often cooked on a stick called a skewer. Many kebabs are made of lamb. They are often served with rice or salad.

INDIA

Hi, my name is Maya. I live in India.

Biryani

Many Indian meals are served with rice. Biryani is rice cooked with lots of different spices, such as coriander, cinnamon, and ginger. It also often includes vegetables and some kind of meat.

Aloo Gobi

Aloo Gobi is made with potatoes, cauliflower, and spices. Its golden color comes from a spice called turmeric. Turmeric is a popular spice in Indian cooking.

turmeric

DID YOU KNOW?

In Hindi, a common Indian language, "aloo" means "potato." "Gobi" means "cauliflower."

JAPAN

Hello! I am Aika. I live in Japan.

Ramen

Ramen is a noodle dish often eaten with chopsticks. The noodles are in a broth and sometimes topped with an egg.

chopsticks

Sushi

Sushi is made with rice. Sushi rice is flavored with vinegar. There are many different types of sushi, such as nigiri and maki. Sushi can be made with fish, vegetables, and seaweed.

maki

nigiri

DID YOU KNOW?

Sushi is often made using <u>raw</u> fish.

A WORLD OF FANTASTIC FOOD

On our tour, we have seen fantastic food from all over our wonderful world. Some of the foods are eaten in many different countries. As people travel, they share foods and learn new things.

Every country has its own fantastic food. Imagine you are a tour guide. If someone came to your country for a visit, what food would you suggest they try?

GLOSSARY

culture	the traditions, ideas, and ways of life of a group of people
dough	a thick mixture used to make bread or pastries
fried	cooked in hot oil
raw	uncooked
spices	things that are used in cooking to add flavor, usually as a powder or seeds
street food	food that is made to be eaten outside on the go
syrup	a thick, sweet liquid
tour	a trip that involves visiting many different places

INDEX

bread 7, 15
cheese 12–13
colors 9, 19
dough 11, 16

fruits 9, 14
limes 6, 8
meat 8–9, 12, 14, 17
nuts 16

potatoes 19
rice 5, 12, 17–18, 21
spices 9, 14, 18–19
vegetables 12, 21